The 3 of Us

(God, Myself, and I)

Author: Desiree' Churchman

Copyright ©2007, by Desiree' Churchman
All rights reserved.
IBSN# 978-0-6151-7425-9
May not copy this book unless you have permission from the author.
The 3 of Us (God, Myself, and I) is a trademark of Desiree' Churchman

All bible scriptures from: The New living Translation Study Bible
Printed in the United States
Published by Desiree' Churchman through lulu.com

Disclaimer:

All views expressed are my own and in no way reflect the opinions of the characters unless noted otherwise.

For more information or questions
Visit my website: www.sweetdreamstxstyle.com

The 3 of Us

(God, Myself, and I)

I would like to first, thank God for giving me the revelation for this book. I also want to thank my husband for supporting me in everything I do!

Love you Tony, my Husband!

~ Table of Contents~

~ My Start (Introduction) ~ pg. 7

~ A Teenager / Per Adult~ pg. 14

~ The Struggle Within~ pg. 43

~ Oh My: "A Young Wife and Mother Fully Loaded"~ pg.70

~ The Vision God Gave Me~ pg. 95

~ My Thoughts, Comments and Encouragements~ pg.103

~ The Author~ pg. 110

~Upcoming Book(s) ~pg. 111

~Notes~ pg.112

~My Start~

(Introduction)

~My Start~
(Introduction)

This book has been on my heart for a while. When it first came to me about two and a half years ago, I thought the title was about my move to Houston, and how my husband and our best friend all met. I said, "How can this be about a Christian lifestyle and a testimony?" I began naming and profiling characters. I even told my pastor about the book, he was excited for me. Therefore, I began to write and write and write. I was on a roll! Not once did I pray and get a full understanding of what I needed to do. Then when I did pray, I still did not listen to God's instructions. All I did was write.

When I reached the third chapter, I just came to a complete stop. "What happened?" I thought. It seemed like I could not remember my life story from one event to the next. "Why?" I asked. "God, if you put this book in my heart, then why am I at a stand still?" I said to myself, "I will finish this later." I was thinking I was too tired to do any more writing. I sat in front of my computer for two and a half days typing. I had a small child that was one years old, and she needed my attention. Again, I avoided listening to the full instructions of God. I could not sit still long enough to hear His instructions. I asked a question, and did my very own answering. Yet, I could pray and wait on God for everything else. I would not make a move in my business, Sweet Dreams TX Style, or any major decision without hearing from God first. I began to think that perhaps God did not want me to write this book. Now I was doubting myself. When doubt comes in, it's the sign of the enemy. I lost all faith in what God told me. I told my husband, "Baby, I think I missed the mark on this one." He told me something that could not have been what he meant to say. "Rena", he said, do you believe that we have lost our Lot from us?" What are you talking about?" I asked. Well, he said, "I have been praying that we loose whatever Lot was to us". In the Bible God told Abraham to go and take his family, but leave Lot. Abraham could not see what reason to leave him, so he brought him along. I was just as lost as a fruitcake in the mail. I just looked up at him and said, "What!" "What do you mean, and what does that have to do with me missing the mark", I replied. Tony said, "baby keep praying and wait on God, before you type another word." Now, he has lost his mind. He was not listening to a word I have been telling him. Now here I go in an up roar. "You have not been listening to me at all! You do not know what I have been sitting here telling you for the last hour, do you? It seemed like it went in one ear and out the other ear." I yelled. Then out of no where I felt the Holy Spirit checking me. I head the words so clearly, "Listen with your heart not with your ears." By this time, the argument that we were having was not an argument with the both of us. It was with myself. Yes, my husband was still there, but not saying a word to me. Tony my husband said, "let us pray and listen to God together. Not about your book, but about our relationship with God to go to another level." My mind was going in circles, because I did not understand at the time what was really happening to us. Therefore, our prayer was to go higher in our worship, praying, giving, praise, and our relationship. Then we sat there and began to hear from God. That was an awesome experience for me. If you have never asked God to get closer to Him and seek His face, this is your time.

This book will not only help you as an adult, but as a teenager, or young adult. What God has place in my heart, July 24, 2006 at 12:00am was this book. After two and a half years, a spoken word came to me. I needed to wait and listen first, for the full instructions. Tonight I was watching Bishop T.D.Jakes, he was speaking about how "***Woman Thou Art Loose***" came about. His message was very touching to me. I felt the Holy Spirit come over me; it released a spoken word to me. I could not wait to start writing.

So as you read this book take notes, highlight or even fold and bend the pages. Your relationship with God is about to go to another Level.

My Prayer and Scripture:

Ps. 23:1-6 (The New Living Translation)

The Lord is my shepherd; I have everything I need. He lets me rest in green meadows; he leads me besides peaceful streams. He renews my strength. He guides me along right paths, bringing honor to his name. Even when I walk through the dark valley of death, I will not be afraid, for you are close beside me. Your rod and your staff protect and comfort me. You prepared a feast for me in the presences of my enemies. You welcome me as a guest, anointing my head with oil. My cup overflows with blessings. Surly your goodness and unfailing love will pursue me all the days of my life, and I will live in the house of the Lord forever.

Pray this Prayer:

Father God, I thank you for my life health, and strength through this journey called life. I thank you for my family Father God. I know as the scripture said, that even thought I will walk in some dark valleys you will be right there. You will keep giving me strength and blessing me Jesus. I will hold on to your everlasting Love forever and ever. I am seeking a closer walk and relationship with you Lord. So as I get closer to you I know that you Father God will protect and comfort me.

In the name of Jesus I pray

                Amen.

Comments/Notes:

_____

_____

_____

_____

_____

~A teenager/Per Adult~

~A Teenager/Per Adult~

As I look back at my teenage years, I think it was great for a moment. I would not say spoiled, but well taking care of. My mother has two daughters including myself. My sister was like night and I was like day. Meaning, we were very different. Not in a bad way, but she liked the town that we lived in and I wanted out. To share a little about my mother, she was a strong single mother. She wanted the best for her girls. She worked two jobs to give us what she believed was the best. As her daughters, we thought it was the best as well. Like most teens and preteens children, you always wanted more. My mother or Aunt Jean to everybody else, kept us in church. She always told us to pray and God will answer. My mother taught us to read the bible and study hard. As a teen it settled into my spirit, but I really did not activate the gift or gifts within. I would go to church and listen neither to the preacher, not hearing nor in taking the word. My mother told me and all the other kids that, we were old enough to start taking notes. I was a great note taker. My bible was highlighted with every color highlighters came in. Did I really make this a life style? Did that really work for me? Yes, to a point, I do believe.

(Flash Back) Saturday nights, I had to go out. Even if it was just to Wal-Mart, I figure at least I am out of the house. I could meet someone I might not have known. That was my way of thinking. I always had someone to tell me; Baby, you look good, or you are very smart. Then on the other hand having people whispering to others, "she must think she is rich, or better than the rest of us." One day in high school during lunchtime, I was in line to receive my lunch tray. A very wealthy guy said to me, " do you know who I am?" The reason for this out burst was to just to cut in line before me. Little did he know that I had a very quick tongue. "What are you doing, I asked." "Do you know who I am?" he stated again. "No, do you know who I am", I stated back to him with an attitude. He stated his name to me and said that his father owns half of this town. I said, "so what, my mother is a hard working woman in this town. Now who is the better person," I stated. Now, to the regular ear and how everyone responded to me, was girl you are crazy. That boy can buy your mama's house. Replying to the crowd in a harsh tone of voice, "Y'all are stupid! Nobody can buy my mama's house!!" I did not care what anybody thought, because I had a different mind set. I told my mom about what happened at school earlier that day and she said, "never let folks run over you because they have a little money." My mothers is a Christian woman, but do to what she was taught she believes she is right. Some of her opinion was according to the word of God plus a little of her own opinion. Now back to the main points of this book. As a teen, I played the piano for about three to four different churches at a time. I loved it! The good points of this were I was able to hear different styles of teaching, and go different places. When I played the piano, I was a very busy lady. I had rehearsals on Mondays, Fridays, Saturdays, and some Sunday's afternoon. Plus, I was in extra curriculum activities at school. Also, I was trying to graduate in three years from high school. My plate was very full. At the age of fifteen, my plate was over whelmed with a lot of things.

    Now you are asking how were you playing for all these

churches and not stay on a positive track with God?" Easy!!! My mind frame was, as long as my sin was not too bad, I could ask for forgiveness and still play. A young lady or child does not get treated well as a musician. I had one church to hire me, they asked how much I wanted them to pay me. I told them, "that really didn't matter to me". Whatever they wanted to give would be fine. I knew you did not have to get paid for something God gave you. What I had was something God gave me and I put it into works. Playing for a church that set in traditions is very hard. I had adults telling me, " We know you are the new piano player, but we do not care. We have been singing at this church longer than you have been on this earth". I swallowed,

"That is fine, but I am here now. You must follow my rules in order for me to play for you." Then I said to myself, "God please help me!" True enough they did to a point. Then before I knew it, I got a phone call after playing for them one year. The person on the other end started to explain to me the reason for this phone call, "we don't need a young child such as yourself that believe that grown folks have to listen to you." So be it, I have lost one job. I really had the attitude that I did not care. My mother told me not to worry about, but I still did. "What did I do WRONG?" "Pray and asked God to bless them and move on," she said.

Teens, I know you are wondering, when did I have time to date or even have fun? Here is how I dated or something like dating. I was always told to date different people. Not sleeping around but dating. Just to see what you like in a young man. I never was taught to pray for a man, so when I dated someone it was a short period of time. I needed to see if he fit my check standard list. If he did not, then I stopped calling and answering his calls. I thought that was the best way. You did not have to explain why and hear well I do not think, and I think we should. So I made the choice for the both of us.

Point of view of a Good Relationship, rather it was a boyfriend/girlfriend or just a friend with someone. Remember these are my very own points, not the word of God. My point of view at that time was, if you wanted to be friends with me, fine. It did not matter, if you were not so cute to someone eyes beauty is in the eye of the beholder. All that matter to me was, if you were kind hearted, told the truth, and was able to put up with my personality. I was the type of person who never met a stranger. I was very loud spoken and did not mind saying what was on my mind. So as a friend of mine, you had to deal with all of that. On the other end, I was also a good listener and believed that I could give you some good advice for your problem. For example, I know not all girls are messy. I know that you can have friends of the opposite sex. One day after school, my mom asked me," who were all those kids I was speaking with outside of my house". Saying to her, "well you know who that is, pointing to the person and stating his name, and that is, stating her name. I named at least ten people. She said ok, but they cannot stay long. I would sometimes ask God to help me choose my friends, but not all the time. In high school, I was on a three-year plan to finish. I wanted out, and out of the school system quick. So, I had a lot of courses to double up and do a lot of summer school classes as well. The spring semester of my junior /senior year of high school, I had a best friend. Well, I had two, but one was a girl and one was a guy. The girl had a crush on my best friend (guy), so I was telling her they should not go together. She asked, "Why, do you want him all for yourself?" "No, not at all, but I know him. I think you should maybe think about it a little longer," I said. "Well, I don't think I have to think at all. If I wanted to go out with him I will," she said. Then to myself I started to pray, "God please make her understand why this should not happen." I did not know what I said came out loud. Then a verbal fight started, and only got worse. For me talking, was just talking. I was the type of person that did not tiff. I would rather be quiet and walk up to you and hit you in the mouth. She made friends with another group of girls, and started hanging out with them. It was fine with me, because I had bigger fish to fry with this guy friend of mine. While in my period of not hanging out with anyone from my high school it gave me time to think. Now, don't get me wrong I just hung out with people outside of my hometown. Then I started to think, did I really have friends, or just associates that like tagging alone with me? Something I had to think about, or was this God's way of moving me? So after a month, the feud had stopped and the semi- truth or what everybody thought was the truth came out. My best friend, the guy, ended up telling her that he did not like her at all, but he liked some one else. Actually, he thought he was in LOVE with another young lady. This was the wrong thing to say to an emotional teenage girl in high school. Finally, it all died down. I know now that as a teen, you must have God all the way in your heart. Then maybe we would avoid a lot of hurt and fights if we would take that time out and truly listen to Him. Can you still have a good friend and be saved? Yes, of course but please, please, let them be a Christian as well, and have a good heart. That is why people flock to me so easily. I have a good heart and enjoyed having a good time. That is the best type of friendship. Now for dating! My last summer in my hometown I met this guy that was charming. I did date other people before him, but it was not the same. We talked over the phone then he fixed me dinner a couple of times. I ask God please let this be the guy for me. I was in LOVE. Again, I did not wait for my answer at all from God. Then the day came. I was at his house and we was all alone. He was talking about how good it felt to be back home. "Where did you go?" I asked. He said, "for the past year I lived out of town. Plus, I also have a little girl now." My heart fell to the floor. I could not deal with baby mama drama. "Nay. Nay. Nay! Are you all right!", he asked. "Oh, yeah I'm fine," I replied. "So when", and then I hesitated for a while. "What's up for tonight?", I asked while changing the subject. "First you seemed a little blown away," he replied. "No, because what happened has happened. There is nothing either one of us can do about it. So what other surprises do you have for me," I asked. "At this time I have given you all the surprises that I can think of," he said. "Good, because I don't need any more for today," I said. "Oh my God what time is it?!," I asked. He said it is about three pm now. "I have to go and get my mom from work," I said with a rushing tone of voice." "Are you coming back?", He questioned. "I do not know about today, why?", I asked. "Well, he said, "I really want you to come back Nay. Do not let what I told you stop you from coming back to see me. I want this relationship to be a good one", in the soft tone of voice he had. "Relationship? Who has a relationship with someone, sir? I do not remember saying that I was in a relationship with someone. Plus I have a boyfriend already," I said. "Oh, really, in a smooth tone of voice. Then why you are not hanging out with him?", he asked. "Because he is at work," I replied quickly. "That's cool with me, if I get all your time and not him, he said. To myself, "only if he knew that I really did not have a boyfriend." So he walked over to me and pulled me close to him. Then said with a smirk on his face, " What if he came by and saw me kissing you?" My heart started beating fast! I said, "nothing, because you will not be kissing me." He said, "please dare me and lets see what will happen." "God please get me out of this so I will not have to explain myself to anybody, why I was kissing a well known bad boy." I said, "Goodbye I will talk to you when I talk to you." I got in the car and said, "Thank you God!" But did God really get me out of something that I put myself into. Deep down inside, I really wanted that kiss. As a teen trying to date, keeping a good reputation for myself and facing all of the challenges was very hard. Now as a parent, you have to allow your child to make some mistakes. If not, they will never know how to rely on God for themselves. Through this period as a teenager, pray that they stay on the right path and really hear from God. Do not get me wrong, as a Christian parent, GET INTO their BUSINESS! Have a talk with them to see where they are mentally and spiritually. Do not go off the deep end when they tell you how they feel, going through something, or how they have fallen short with God. Try to stay calm and be open minded with them, but still know that you are the parent and they are the child. You are <u>not</u> their BEST friend! A Christian parent is there to help guide and give Godly advice. As a teen, you must realize you are still the child. You also have them too understand they can come to you, the parent instead of the world. The enemy will come in and try to take their minds away. As for me, my mom really kept tabs on me. Always asking me what is going on with me. I opened up to a point I thought my mother could handle for a mother daughter relationship. I thought it was the best relationship ever. She would tell me, "Baby sometimes you have to leave some folks alone, because they see were you are going and they don't want you to go there." So, "Nay you just pray to God and let Him guide you", she would always say. (I love my mom!) There was one problem I thought. Great advice, but will I listen? That was the problem. I would pray then come to my very own understanding. For one week, I prayed and did not talk to the young man. It felt like years had gone by. I replayed all the relationships that I had with other young men in my mind. Trying to see why it did not last like normal relationships. I did not want to be in a long-term relationship, because it seemed too committed. Some people would say I picked up the characteristics or even the spirit of a guy. That is who I hung out with and was around all the time. My cousin and his friends took me around as a cousin or a little sister. I saw and heard first hand on, what, when, where, and how, and how many times they had messed over and used women. So, by that I was protecting myself from men hurting or miss using me. I often talked to one of my favorite teachers. She told me, love can be good, when I find the right one. I responded as, "I think I have fallen in love." "Nay, I really believe this is just puppy love", she stated. "Think about it for a moment, you will be moving in three months and you really don't need to string someone along", she said. "How would I be stringing him along? I haven't even told him I was moving out of town yet", I replied softly. "Well, baby you might want to start taking that into some considerations. A young man like that might want a long term relationship," she answered. "But I need him right now, and in more ways than one", I stated. "What are you saying Nay? Do you want to have sex with him?", she asked. I looked her straight in her eyes and said, "Well kind of. Does that make me a bad person?," I asked with concern. "No, but that is a lot of responsibility that a young single lady not married should not want to take right now. You have so much ahead of you. You have school and things to complete before sex should come in your mind. I mean you should not act on it," she explained. Could this be God trying to tell me something through her? Maybe I should just sit and talk to him before I start jumping off the deep end. "Thanks for talking and helping me clear and straighten out some thoughts in my head." I told her. That night when he called me, I took the phone call. "Where have you been?", he asked. "I have been around town," I responded. "So what's up with you not stopping by my house anymore?", he questioned. "Well, you know, since I have a boyfriend I really didn't need to stop by your house or talk to you over the phone," I said. "So why are you talking to me now?" he asked. "Because, I was bored and I really did not have a lot to do. So since you were the last person to call, I figure why not, just talk to you," I said. "Your comments and the way you say them are going to get you in trouble one day," he said softly. I laughed! With laughter in my voice, I said, "then you should just hang the phone up so you will not have to hear my comments." (Laughing), "girl, girl, I must really like you. To be honest I would not take that from anybody else", he proclaimed. "Guess what?, I'm not the regular girl from around the way," I replied back with an attitude. "You are right about that Nay. You are cute, well I should say a lot more beautiful than they are," he said. I laughed and said, "Dude your game is very weak." Wherever you moved from, their game must have been weak as well?", I told him. He laughed and stated, "For someone that is so small you have some big TALK!" "Yeah, I know and you are not the first to tell me that at all," I replied. A week or so had past by without just talking over the phone. Then one night while we were on the phone he asked, "Would you stop by here when you drop your mother off at work?" "Yeah that's cool, no problem. What's up?," I asked. "Nothing, just would like to put the face with the voice," he stated softly. "Oh really, but listen to me and hear me, I am not up for no lame tricks or games you are trying to run," I said. "I'm not here for game Nay, I just want to see you and talk with you. I really enjoy talking with you over the phone. I just need to put your face back with the voice," he said. "Oh, so now you have forgotten what I looked like?, I questioned. "No, but I just wanted to see you girl!", he said in a louder tone of voice. "Are you raising your voice at me?," I stated. "Not at all, but may I, please see you?," in a sweet soft voice, he said. "Alright, I will stop by in the morning," I replied. "My goodness, why did you have to give me such a hard time?," he asked. "I don't know, but it was fun for me to see how far I could push you," I told him. That morning I dropped my mom off at work and went over his house. Seriously, we sat outside and I was glad. We laughed and talked about things happening around town. More like playing catch up with one another. I enjoyed the out come of this. I prayed and my prayer was answered, at least I thought. The key thing was did I pray for the right thing? We must teach our teens how to pray and what to pray for. The day came that I thought I was so egger to have, but at the same time I did not want this day to happen. He said, "let's go inside and have some breakfast, but we did not go to the kitchen." After everything was over, I went blank. My mind was in a daze. I could not believe I had done such a thing. I enjoyed it, but I knew it was so wrong. I expected something just to happen. Like the sky to crack open, and for God Himself to hit me over the head. That did not happen at all! I never prayed against lust at all. I really did not know, that is what I should have prayed against. All I knew was to pray for things that you did want to happen, and things that you did not want to happen. I did not know to pray against my flesh. Now, don't start thinking what did her pastor teach her. He taught all that he knew to teach. Once the word of God has been taught, it is now up to the teen to put it into action. Yet, we as Christian have to stop putting blame on others for what they might not have been taught, in order to teach the upcoming generations to come. What they have learned and even what we have learned is to help us to get through our journey of life. The season that we are in, we have learned to hear from God on what we need to overcome at that time. "If one learned all that is needed to know for everyone's season; how will one live through and learn through their season lessons". So now, I'm looking funny while I put my clothes back on. He spoke to me very softly and asked, "Are you ok?" "Uh mm, Uh mm, yeah, why you asked," I stated in an uneasy voice. "For one, you sound like something went wrong. Was it not what you expected?", he asked. "Well, it was even better than what I expected, but it was not supposed to happen. I am a young Christian woman and I have fallen short. What will the church say? Can you tell me that," I said with anger behind my voice. "Listen to me and hear me!", he said with power behind his voice. I looked up and sat on the bed. "Nay, you are a beautiful young lady and these past few months I could not get you out of my mind. I'm the type of person that doesn't let people or women get close to me." I think all women are out to get something from me. Every date that I have been on or even relationships they (women) have used me. I really like you, but I don't want you doing anything that makes you feel bad. I said all of this so you can understand how I feel," he told me. In my heart, I knew he was not running game. For some reason it seemed as though it was coming from his heart. So I asked him, "Where do we go from here?" "I don't know, but I know I want to be with you, he said tenderly. "Alright, so I understand that, but I don't know how to fix my relationship with God," I asked. "Well how about this, ask God to forgive you and ask your boyfriend to do the same," he said with a smile. "Don't worry about the boyfriend, because I don't have a boyfriend," I said with a small half smile on my face. He started to laugh! I asked, "what is so funny!?" He kept laughing harder and harder. Then in between laughing and taking a breath he said, "I was afraid that I was going to have to kick his butt." Then I started laughing and said, "No you weren't because, I would have hated it if you would have gotten beat up, if I had a boyfriend." So we just kept laughing and making jokes. Would this be a beautiful time to lead someone to the Lord? Yes, it would, but sometimes it's not how it happens. The relationship grew and I slowly walked away from God. Parents calm down! You pray your child or children stay covered by the blood and keep praying for them. Do not blame yourself, because one, they are at the age of understanding and knowing what is right or wrong. At this time point, begin to challenge them with the word of God. Use the word of God not only to challenge them but to teach them. There is nothing new under the sun, the names of the sin only CHANGED, that's all. Teens believe that as a parent you do not know what you are talking about because you are seasoned and have learned and gained wisdom. That is not true; parents remember that the things you went through as a teen were in a different day and time. So much has changed. So what was rare to you then, is ok for teens now. The children don't look at it as surprising if you find a gun or have a gun. Some even think having three or four kids while in high school is of the norm. So, with the word challenge them since they don't really want to listen to you. In addition, if your church has teen ministries go to the teen minister and have them talk to the child. Someone different can reach the child better than the parent. Teens believe, you as the parent don't know anything. Please remind the teen, this is your house and they must follow your rules. With teenagers, you sometimes will have to take them to the word. Just show them the word and line up the things you are telling them with the word. Also, let them know you and your spouse are there for them. Now you have done your part well, but let God help you guide them the rest of their spiritual paths. The two months of our relationship got serious. Then the night came for me to say goodbye. It was going to be very hard for me. The whole time, I still failed to bring the subject up to him. I called his house and asked if I could come over. I waited and the phone rung, seemed like forever. "Hello", in a very low voice coming from the other end. "Hey," with a shaky voice, I said. "Hey you, what's going on," he replied. "Are you sleep, because I need to talk to you?", I asked. "No, sweetie just relaxing, lets talk," he replied. Uh mm, I started to say. "No, Uh mm, means something is not going so well," he said. "May I come over?", I asked. "Sure come over," he said. "Give me ten minutes and I will be there," I said. I heard my voice starting to crack. I hung up the phone and asked my mom could I use her car to go handle some business. "What business Rena?", my mom asked. That is what my mother called me when I am bothering her, in trouble, or saying something crazy to her. "Well, I need to say good bye to some people before I live in the morning", I said. "Rena, don't be gone long because we have to leave early in the morning", she replied in a serious voice. When that happens, it means she is not joking around. "OK!", I yelled while grabbing the keys and leaving in a hurry. I wanted to get out the yard before she could change her mind. Playing in my mind was all my home girls or so calls friends that were in my ear about, "girl, this is a summer fling. This won't last when you move, you just need to tell him that you are moving." With all those things running in my mind, I started to cry. I know this was for real. I got there and it was like he heard me drive up and get out the car. I was glad that it was dark outside, so he could not see I was crying. "Well, uh mm, uh mm", I said with a crackly voice.

"Come here, what is wrong with you?", he asked in a worried voice. He held me tight and I started getting myself together. "I will be leaving in the morning for school. I will only return some weekends and holidays", I said slowly. "What are you saying Nay?", he asked in an unsure voice. "I'm saying that I am leaving. I'm sorry that I did not tell you I was moving," I said all of this in-between the tears. My tears flowed like a rushing river. "Nay, with a crackly voice. I'm going to miss you like crazy. I don't know what to do at this time." he said. "Please don't hate me, because I wanted to tell you but every time was not the right time," I said. "No, no, don't worry about that", he said and held me tighter. "You go to school and do what you have to do. Just know that I love you!" he said with a sad tone of voice. My heart fell on the floor! I could not believe what I just heard. "I, I love you too." I said. This only felt right for me to say. I did not know what love was or felt like. Was it the sex we had or was having talking to me at this very moment? The enemy had me so wrapped in his hand I did not know anything any more. All I knew was, I was loosing someone that really cared about me and

I did not know if I felt the same way or not. I thought why not, because it feels right for me to respond back this way. By this time, we're both crying. "Here take this and hold it close to you. Everytime you get lonely or think of me you hold it close to you", he said. I cleared my water works and looked down and it was a ring. "Wow! I don't know what to say", I stated back to him. "Say you will take it with you", he said with hope in his voice. "I'm not marrying you! For one I'm young and have a lot to do", I responded. "Nay, baby I know girl. I just want to have something", he said to me. "Let me think a minute, because I don't want to make the wrong mistake" I responded back. "Please just take it for me, for our love for each other. Not making any marriage commitments or even the promising thing", he said. I was just standing there with his eyes looking into mine. Here I go calling on God. "God please at this time, what should I say?" I don't want to say the wrong things. "God if you get me out of this, I will do better", I said to myself. Why at this time do we all call on God? We have not prayed, praised, or study His word at all. Now we want Him to show up and show out! Why, when we have not done a thing to give Him glory or praise. That is just like for someone to go to the store and asked the clerk to give them credit and they have never been in that store before. Those clerks really don't know who they are at all. The clerk is just seeing them for the first time in the store. Or the clerk has not seen or heard from them in months or years and they still owe on their last bill. That credit has worn off or they have used it all up. Don't laugh because we all know it is the true. We like to misuse and abuse everything in this day and time. We want everything right now and in a hurry. We're a microwave society. Now put God as the clerk, but this clerk has a bigger and better heart. Now the enemy has stepped into my ear and I go ahead and go alone with the plan he the enemy has for me at the time. "I will take it for our LOVE," I said softly. Did I listen to God? Alternatively, just react to the problem and emotions that was at hand.

    Therefore, I left and went home. My eyes were opened after leaving the next morning, to bigger, opened, and deeper waters. I always had control in the shallow waters. Will my walk get back on the right track? Will I realize I had lost my walk with

God? How will one know that they are off track if they don't know if they were never on track? All these things were on my mind, but at the time, I felt like I have time to work all that out before judgment day. I thought since I was in a big city I should get the feel and hang of things. Everybody else at college was partying and having fun, why couldn't I. Changing and growing in my life as I go from a teen to adult hood. So the time was going by me so fast, and I was meeting so many different people all the time. My puppy love relationship I saw was going down hill. The long distance was a killer for the both of us. I was not honest in my letters to him on how I felt. I just could not let him know that I was sad all the time. I did not want to hurt his feelings at all, plus my heart was to kind for that. I always put others before me no matter what I was feeling or going through. I believed that it will last if I just keep writing. Not really saying, I feel lost, afraid, and all alone. So over a years time period it slowly faded away. Before my eyes, I felt like my life went up side down. Plus I really did not pray or study the bible like I did before. I HAD NO COVERING! Where do I go from here? Do I rely on man to left me up? My mind was blocked and far away from God. Shopping, and spending money to make me happy was all that mattered. I was going to work in the afternoons getting off in the wee hours of the night, just so, my mind would not be still just on me. When I got home from work, I studied, then up early to go to school the next morning. Let me rephrase that, and say up in a few hours to go to school. I was lost in the spirit and in the natural. Where does one turn to now?

My prayer and Scripture:

John 8:12-16 (The New Living Translation)
Jesus said to the people; "I am the light of the world. If you follow me, you won't be stumbling through the darkness, because you will have the light that leads to life." The Pharisees replied, "You are making false claims about yourself!" Jesus told them, "These claims are valid even though I make them about myself. For I know where I came from and where I am going, but you don't know this about me. You judge me will all your human

limitations, but I am not judging anyone. And if I did, my judgment would be correct in every respect because I am not alone – I have with me the Father who sent me.

Pray this prayer:

Father God, thank you for showing me the light. Help guide me and to stay on track. Thank you for not letting me fall to the wayside. Help me stay focus in your word and in my prayer life. Help me remember that I need to lean on you and you only Father God. Not to relay upon man, but you Jesus will provide for me. Let me not judge one, not knowing what they are going through. I pray that everyone that comes in contact with me, will see Your light Father. In the name of Jesus I pray

Amen

Comments/Notes:

_____

_____

_____

_____

~The Struggle Within~

~The Struggle Within~

Here I was a hot mess on the inside. I tried to go to church, but I still felt something was missing. Knowing what it was, do I fix it by going to Christ, or look for a club, party, or a new boyfriend? Maybe whatever else I could find to keep me running. I stopped working out and as a wise tale LET MYSELF Go! No, not my spirit, but my physical appearance. I never had enough money to do all the things I wanted to do, like most young people that get out on their own, we don't realize what bills mommy and daddy had to pay. We think it was OK, because we had everything that we needed at our parents' house. Young people I have a rude awakening for you. IT IS NOT EASY!! If you don't work, you don't eat. I am not talking spiritual but in the real world. It is cold and hard out there. Therefore, every time you smart off to your parents and say, with an attitude, "I can't wait to get my own place to stay, apartment, or whatever." Yes, you can. The rules at mama and daddy's house are not that bad after all. So please wait to grow up and listen to them, because they know what they are talking about. By the time I paid my bills and wanting to shop, I forgot that I might need food to eat as well. At the time, I was thinking those red DKNY shoes will look fly with those new DKNY red pants and tight white shirt that I just got. Then the red purse to go with it, I must have it. Then go home eating fruit cocktail in a can with a ham sandwich. I thought I was living the American young persons dream. My own apartment and I can go and come as I please. Then I wanted to do so much more. I kept wondering what will happen next. So my roommate that I was very close to asked me, what was up with me. I told her that I was just feeling lonely. "Girl, all you need to do is go running, shopping, and find a little cutie pie and things will get better." she said. "Yeah, I guess so!" I said. "I will hook up with you later. Alright, out," she said. "Out (other words goodbye)," I responded back to her. Many nights of studying, working, and crying myself to sleep. Thinking how did I get like this? As a young adult, you have to transfer properly, spiritually and naturally from a teen, pre adult, then a young adult. If you don't have all the things spiritually lined up, your natural part will lack. You have to feed your spirit man so it will grow. Look at it as if it was a baby. If you don't feed the baby then it will fight to live as long as it can. Then the baby will soon die. This is the same with your spirit man. So there I was debating with the wrong things. I knew what was needed to be done, but still I did not make a move. I just needed to say, "Father here I am, fill my heart with your love." Before I could get those words out, I heard the door open and close to my apartment. My roommate was back. "Nay, are you still here?", she called out to me. "Yes, in a low tone of voice. "Why, what's up?," I asked. "Hold on I'm back on the phone", she said. "Listen to his voice," she said quietly while handing me the phone. "Who?", I questioned. "You stupid", she stated. A nice sound that had warmth in it came from the other end. "Hello", the voice said. I gave her the phone back. So they started to talk. She was sitting in my room on the floor, and I asked her how long will she be on the phone. She said not long. Then she said, "He wants to speak with you". "Hey", with a crackly or shaky voice, I responded. "This is not", and before I could get the name out of my month, she said, "you should know better than that". The conversation went on into the wee hours of the night. Right before I got off the phone, I asked him did he want to hook up on Friday and go to the movies with some of us. He said, "Yeah, why not, it sounds cool". "Thank you God for sending someone to me", I said to myself. I was rejoicing. My spirit or should I say my feelings were brought back to speed. Now we all know that I have not prayed to God for anything, but in my mind, I thought God had sent me someone to cheer me up. Maybe that was all I needed right then and there. I really did not have to rededicate my life to God, but He still came through for me. Now why would God do that and I have not been connected with Him for over a year. But we fail to remember that God has a plan for us weather we know it or not. God did not forget my prayer that I had asked for my mate to come forth. It did not come when I wanted it, but God sent him right in time just for me. So now I had only one other small thing that I was dealing with. That was a Soul ties or made convent with someone.

    We as Christian really don't talk to our teens about sex. We beat around the bush and tell them not to do it. Why not, a teen is thinking. You have not shown them in the word of God why not. As an adult, we treat sex as a bad sore and we cannot touch or talk about. I never looked at having sex before marriage this way before, until I was taught. Then God gave me a revelation to teach all teens that I come in contact with about premarriatal sex. I know this might have made a difference in my life if I knew about this before hand. Once you have slept with that person before you are married, a little piece of them stays with you. They have left some type of mark as well as you have left a mark with that person. Meaning, your soul has broken convenient with that person and the two of you have become one. But in the natural, you just get up and go home or roll over and go to sleep. That's why you are supposed to be married so you can become one with each other. This is whom God has placed on earth for you and the two of you are suppose to fulfill a purpose in this journey. So this was my struggle. I had to pretend to let all that go to move on quickly. So that Friday came and I was getty all day. The doorbell rung and my heart started to rush. I opened the door and OH MY GOD it was Him......!! A loud laughter came from my mouth like I cannot believe it is you. "Do I know you?" He said. "Well, just come in here", I said in an East Texas accent. I calmed down to help him remember where I saw him at. He said, "Well, I kind of remember, but I don't remember". "I'm, Nay and these are my roommates. You already know one of the ladies". Let me describe this man to you. He was a tall dark complected, gorgeous smile, nice teeth, which was a plus to me. I did not like an ugly smile or bad teeth. I don't know why, but that told me that if you took time to keep your teeth up then you take time out to keep your self up. Back to my hunk, he was dressed nice and neat, ladies a young man that wore a built correctly and pants fitted him very, very nicely! I was just in heaven. Then the soft-spoken voice he had would have made you just melt. But I always have to play calmer than I really am. I never showed how I really felt because I thought guys would take advantage of you. Some will, but you cannot hold that against every man. For one, my heart had been broken once, so I knew that I did not want that to happen again. "Are you ready to go?" he asked. "I'm waiting on you", I said. Then out of the blue, my roommate asked me to step into her room and started asking me what I thought of him. I said, "Well", and I don't know why I did not want to give her the full 411, but I told her briefly, "he has a nice smile and he is dressed very well". "Girl, I told you! So let's go", she said. "Tony, are you ready for the second time now," I asked. "Yes, I am, just waiting on you", he said with a soft tone of voice. We finally go to the movies, and we are laughing and talking in the parking lot. It seemed like we already knew each other very well. Then we waited on my friends to see what movie they were going to see, but I did not want to see what they was seeing. We bought our tickets that we wanted to see and went inside. I felt relaxed with him. We held hands until we found the right seats. He was so funny to me. He told jokes to no end while the movie was playing. I laughed and felt like my joy was restored. After the movies, he went back to my place. He started to drink. This was not water at all. I could not believe this. How could God send me someone that was an alcoholic! That was not cool at all. But my heart still jumped for joy. We talked until we both fell asleep. "Good morning", I said with a happy tone of voice. "What time is it", Tony asked. "Oh, it is about nine or ten in the morning", I told him. "Not good, wake me up after twelve", he said in a sleepy tone of voice. "What? God you have to be punishing me?" I said to myself. I'm trying to get my life together and then here comes Mr. More Problems, a drinker and a lazy person all in one. I was just blown away by the type of person God had put in my life. Ladies that is the first thing we start doing as women, judging and thinking God has messed our lives up. Not thinking maybe God has put that person in your life so that you can help them get to the next level. You never know that a kind word as well as you just taking time out with that person can make a difference. Now I had prayed to God for a mate, but when someone came along, I did not want to take them and the flaws. I just wanted a great guy, but he had to be perfect. Don't judge so quickly Ladies, wait and see what a beautiful butterfly you might have. You might have enter during the caterpillar stages of their life. You will have to let God work out what He has planned for them and you. Therefore, I had to take a step back and think a minute. I started to think maybe it is for a reason. I should not be judging against someone as SEXY as he was. I will pray about this small problem later. Well, later never came for me. So when Tony finally got up we started to talk. I asked him questions about himself. "So how have you been doing?" Well, I mean as far as life and your journey?", I asked. It's alright," he said. Then he went on to say, I started school at SFA and completed the rest at home." With a small laughter in my voice I said, "You had me going for a while, because I was going to ask you what your major is. I did not know you were going to say that." "Well, you know I try," he said in a smooth voice. "So what's up with you?" he asked me. "I am going to school to be a Pharmacist," I responded back to him. "So you are going to be selling drugs", he asked with laughter in his voice. "Yeah, I guess you can say that", I said laughing. "A legal drug dealer," he said. "Wait, not like that," I said laughing! So we were in my room sharing back and forth on points of our lives. I shared a little bit about my ex-boyfriend at that time. I did not want to share too much about the past. I told him, "We could be friends Tony, but I don't think we should have a real relationship just yet." "That's cool," he said with a smile on his face. "I feel the same way", he said. "Why don't you want to get in a relationship?" I asked. "I don't think I am ready for that just yet. He said, "Since I am a lady's man." A burst of laughter came from my mouth. "Do what?" I said. You heard me! A lady's man," he said with joy. "I am one of the smoothest men out there," he continued to say. I was laughing until tears came out of my eyes. "Please stop, because I can not take it anymore," I said. "Are you for real Tony?" I asked in an unsure voice. Now ladies, please stop and take a breather, because that was a lot right there. Sometimes you just have to dig deeper to see if someone is joking. Now with his looks and personality it could be very easy for women to like him a lot. Tony seemed to give you want you needed to hear at the right times. He could walk in a room and lighten the mood. A funny outgoing guy like this could get a young lady very easy. If you feel unsure about something, ask and let them know the type of person you are. Don't play a game with them, be up front and honest. Sometimes we take things to serious and it shouldn't be at all. Lighten up and take things slowly, plus God put them in your life for a reason. Seek God on what direction you need to take. Now with me I am a very different young lady. I had this one thought on my mind that when I wanted something I must have it. Now don't think different of me now, because you have read to far to stop now. Plus I have a great since of humor. So now back to the main story. I stated, "I hope you are kidding me." Softly and a smooth tone of voice he responded, "Yeahhh." I shook my head, still trying to stop the laughter. "Anyway, I am glad we got all of that out of the way," I said with laughter still in my voice. We hung out and talked over the phone for the next few months.

    Thinking to yourself if this is Godly or not? Let's simply talk about Christian dating. Only a few words keep it clean, go home before 9 pm or no later than 10 pm, no touching all over. Look at it this way young people, God is your Father and he is watching you at all times. Just like in the natural, a young lady has a Father that seems scary, well look at God the same way both male and female. Now theses are a few words from the book of Rena. Some times people can go over board saying I cannot date because Jesus himself did not date. I believe dating will help build character for you. You don't have to do anything that will disrespect yourself or even make you feel like you have gotten off the path of God. Please, teens if you want to date ask and even talk to your parents. Make sure that you all are on the same page. Remember as a teen you must follow the rules and guide- lines that your parents or guardians have laid on the line for you. Parents please talk and go into great detail on the rules and concerns that you might have. This way the teen will understand what you expect of them. Don't shut them out and expect them to know what you want, and don't want them to do. Be willing, open and understanding with them. This will make things go a lot smoother in the future.

    Now back to the story. Then I met one of Tony's good friends. Tony had told me that he favored a rapper. I did not believe it until I saw him for myself. "Hi, I am Nay and you must be Joe." "Yes, I am Joe," he replied. So all three of us hung out and became very close. I saw Joe as a brother to me. The two of them, (Tony and Joe) would come over to the apartment as much as they would like. I really liked Tony a lot and when you like someone you want to see them all the time. But all three of us grew together like small children enjoying life. My roommates started to act kind of funny or weird. It was three young ladies in a three-bedroom apartment. This was a bomb ready to go off. By that time, my life was just about inside out. I had not picked up my bible in a while. I had started an intimate relationship with Tony. I knew my spirit man had become very quite. I had not stood up for what I believed in before. I never said; let's have a nice Christian relationship. Questions started rolling in my mind. Nay what are you doing? What are you trying to do with yourself? These questions kept running in my mind. It felt like everything was flashing before my eyes. Before I knew it things seemed better, but really were not. I started to walk around the block to ease tension. I believed as a young adult you should not be so stressed, overwhelmed, and not sure if you are right with the Lord. Being right with God should be the number one thing you should be real sure of. This walk I believe should not be stressful to you. Yes, you will go through some trials and some test, but not stressed at all. Also, you should not have worry or doubt in your heart. The word of God quotes in, Mark 11:23, "I assure you that you can say to this mountain, "May God lift you up and throw you into the sea," and your command will be obeyed. All that's required is that you really believe and do not doubt in your heart." When those two, doubt and worry come into your heart, your blessings will stop flowing. God wants you to rely on Him and not yourself or man. You have to have that very clear before you get upset with yourself. Don't worry; you do not have to be perfect if you are just coming into this walk. I know it will not be perfect once you are in this walk. You will get off track, but you ask for forgiveness and get back on! So now, for months I still don't know were I was headed too. I knew that number one, GET BACK on track with God. Then the second thing was to finish school. After a while, my language changed. My body language changed, and I did not want the church over taking me. Meaning what good effects money, number of people, and many of the people judging me. Now I am really missing home. I was crying inside and outside. Tony walked in my room one day and I was crying. "What is wrong?", with a deep concern, he asked.

"Well, I don't think I need to share all of this with you right now." I responded back. "Talk to me about as much as you can. Just get it all out," he stated. So I started to share with him. "I am lonely," I said wiping my face. "I am here," he said in a very soft voice. Then he put his arm around me. I cried even harder. I don't know, but all I know is what I feel is real. So again, I say, "I am lonely," I said to him. With an upset voice Tony asked, "You mess him?" Slowly not knowing we were on two different people. "Yes, I do and I want things to be right," I said. Tony stood up and replied, "I knew it was not over with you and him. That is why I did not want to make any commitments to you or anybody," he said with an angry tone of voice. "Sit down boy, I am talking about God," I said quietly. "With God, all of this is over God and not your ex.", he said. I looked up and saw a small smile on his face. "Oh, I am very sorry, I just thought you meant," and before he could finish a loud noise came from the living room. The other two roommates were fussing about something. I told him, "Just don't say anything and it will just stop." I have deeper problems to deal with than two grown women arguing over some orange juice. I just want out of this apartment, because this is not my cup of tea. I like peace within and out. I don't like the tension and the attitude that is in this house. I think, because I stay quite for so long then I blow up like a bomb. Which, holding my anger inside is not good at all. Then all those questions came back to mind. God, why me at this time? Please send me my mate. So as a young adult, we want to have peace with God and also still do what ever we want in the world. Trying to be all grown up without God will not work. God is our only way. As young adults, if we realize that first, some things we would not have to go through at all. Also, God put certain people in our lives so that they can share wisdom with us. But nine times out of ten we do not receive, the wisdom that has came forth to us. Sometimes the word or advice will be right on time, and we blow it off as nothing. In reality, we really need to embrace it and lay pride aside. When pride rise up that is something deadly. That's why Satan himself got cast down out of heaven. He let pride rise up with in himself and wanted to battle God. All of that said, our spirit man gets smaller and smaller, and it will never grow. Young adults you will have to make that decision of choosing the world or God. Most believe that once you get saved all the fun is suppose to stop. WRONG!!! You can still have fun and enjoy yourself as a young adult. Look at it this way, you don't loose much, but you gain so much more. My struggle got worse day by day. I even started to take shots of alcohol. I heard the voice of God saying, **"All you have to do is come to me and I will fill your heart**." I did not listen because, I choose not to at the time. My money was right and it seems as if the friends that I had were there for me in my time of need. Months went by faster that I can count. In between times, one roommate moved out and we never spoke again. I had mostly hurt in my heart because she had the chance to escape the drama and I did not. I really believed that since I did not know much about the city, and I did not have anywhere to go, so I stayed there. Just a single lost of a friend added another weight to me. If you ever loose a friend then your heart is broken, but God put people in your life for a time and a season. Then all you have to do is pray and talk to God. Trust me He will listen when no one else will. Why should you fight or fix a battle that has already been won for you? For an example, you have an older sister or brother and they tell you that I already took care of that for you. But you jump up and try to fight or fix the problem. Who are you fighting and why? The older sibling has done that already. The same thing with God, He has already done it for you. Just give Him the praise for it.

    I noticed as time went by, the enemy kept attacking me. I had nothing to fight back with. I know you are thinking that I have been in church all the way up until now, something should be still there. Yes, but if you don't exercise it enough it will go away. Just like body fat, you get rid of it, but once you stop the healthy foods and all the exercises then the fat comes back. Make the fat the enemy and make the healthy food the word of God (Bible), then make the exercises God. It all works the same way. Finally, as the years have flown by, I am still in school and in a small one-bed room apartment with my boyfriend. I know we were in a big sin. My mother fusses to know end to me about it. My mother told me, "That is not how a young Christian woman should act or live." I could not get mad, because it was the truth. Tony and I would talk about how we could fix things to try and make everything right. Now I was thinking to myself that I have too much on me right now, and we have time. We mention marriage but did not want to take the action of it. I believe it was coming one day, but now the time was too soon. Then I started to pray again. The praying started after my boyfriend told me that we could not have sex together any more. I thought he had lost his mind. At that point, I thought we was moving further away. I did not know that it only made us grow closer together. So Tony had changed. He did not want to drink that much and his language changed, and just everything about him had changed. Not for the worse but for the better. I was amazed at him, and by him. Changing made me want to change for the better as well. We started to have conversations that were different. We talked about children and how many we wanted, also about MARRIAGE. So I started praying a little every day. At this time in your life, all God wants is for you to come back to Him. I was kind of tired of the life that I was living. Not knowing Tony was in the same kind of fight I was in. I remember the day so clearly when I changed my life around. I just got up and started to pray and confess to God. "I surrender to you Lord, I don't know any other way. Show me the directions I need to go in. I need You right now in my life! Show me if Tony is the right man, I need to be with. Is he the mate you have here on earth for me? Show me some signs. Please forgive me for turning away from You. Now I am turning everything over to you right now and forever." At that point, I got Saved. Young adults when you read this you should take advantage of your chance to get saved if you are not. It is not hard at all. It is totally up to you, God is waiting. Don't blow it off thinking you have all the time in the world. Don't think you have to have everything together because you will not. This is why God wants you with Him so that He can help you work those things out for the best. The whole point of coming to Christ is so He will help you get your life in order. Just confess with your mouth and believe in your heart that you shall be saved, according to the word of God. So now, I am saved. What should I do now at this point? After I had done that, my eyes opened to some things. Then I had notice that Tony had changed for the best. Before I thought, he was just loosing interest in me and trying to move on. He never said he had rededicated his life back to God. But I did notice is speech and the little things about him had changed. My eyes were just covered and I did not want to see the change. He came to me and said until we get married will not have any sexual activities any more. I said, "Yes you are right." Now remind you that we still live in a small one-bed room apartment, but we have made up in our minds that this will work.

  A month went by and out of nowhere, Tony asked me to marry him. I did not take him serious at first, because I was watching my UPN Monday night shows. Then he said it again and I was shocked. My eyes got watery and I said, **"YES",** with a joyful tone and excitement to my voice. We hugged and I cried. God gave me the sighs that I needed. Stop and let me explain these signs. Mine will be different from yours, because of what I had asked for. My signs were as follows: 1.) Relationship with the Lord. 2.) Treat me with the up most respect. 3.) A vision of were he wanted his family or us to go in life (this was one of the most important to me) 4.) What our purpose was or ministry. Let me go back and say that Tony was a playful, joking, sports minded person. So for me to see him very serious was a great thing. Some of us as young women want a certain man. We build our minds up that this man must have the followings before I have a relationship with him or even think about marrying him. Ladies please check the following that apply to you and see where you stand at this point.

Goal List for the Number Man in My life – Test

1.) A car

2.) Some where to stay that is his own – house/ apartment

3.) MONEY

4.) A six figure job

5.) Take care of me

6.) Give me what I want out of life

7.) Love to Travel

8.) Tall / Short

9.) In great shape

10.) Very, Very Sexy

Those are some of the top ten things we as women want. Some of us even say a saved man, but nine out of ten will ask for the ten given above. So when God sends us our mate, we let him pass us by because it did not fit our LIST. Women we are WRONG! You must pray and seek God, but remember the word of God say, when a MAN finds as wife he finds a good thing. Now that all of this is happening to me and the enemy comes at me very strong. He hits me with a world wind. But right in the mist of all the storms the enemy threw at me, I stood still and let my God work. Then as I looked back over the past years, I thanked God for bringing me out of the struggle with myself. I am not saying that it is all over, but that level of struggle is over. Please note that "forgiveness is not easy, but a small Process". So once you get into the process you seek God even more to help you through, that's what I had to do. I had the biggest problem with anger towards people. If I did not have a good explanation from that person to help me understand why they were hurting me, I just kept that hurt and turned it into anger towards that person. I thank God that I have over came that struggle. Even thought I am still working some of the rough edges out in that area, I can say that I'm getting there. Don't get me wrong it is not easy, but I know my reward will be greater in the end of the process. So I say to you from experience: "Hang in there. Follow through with the process of whatever you are in. Remember God is on your side. Don't give up, because you may be right at the end of your breakthrough". Stop the struggle within yourself and let God take all of that for you. Fight and keep fighting the enemy. But always remember God is on your side and the battle is not yours. Too stop the struggle within you, Run to Christ and all of that will end through a process.

My scripture and Prayer:

Ephesians 4:32 (The New Living Translation)
"Instead, be kind to each other, tenderhearted, forgiving one another, just as God through Christ has forgiven you."

Pray this Prayer

Father, forgive me I know I have fallen short. Let me turn all my headaches over to you. Help me learn how to let these people that I have bundle up within my spirit go. I know it will not happen over night Father God. Ease my pain away. As I let them go and forgive them, send your ministering angles to me and have them to surround me. Protect me and guide me Father as I go down this pathway. I know Father that this is a process that I must go through. I am seeking to be closer to you. Stress, doubt, and worry you must flee right now in the name of Jesus. I am giving my all unto you God. Block my ears and eyes from negative things in this season. Let me be able Father to know the people you want around me. Father all the people that I forgive and let go, touch their hearts as well Father. Let them feel the weight that I have put upon them be lifted. Even if I was wrong, Father let those that I have hurt or offended in any kind of way to forgive me as well. Let this process be used to Glorify you and only you God. In the name of Jesus I pray, Amen

Comments/Notes:

_____

_____

_____

_____

~Oh My: "A Young Wife and Mother Fully Loaded"~

~Oh My: "A Young Wife and Mother fully Loaded"~

Praise the Lord!! We finally got married! What all will change now? Do the bills get better or worse? How do I pray for my husband when he has pushed my last button? What do I do when I get so angry and want to leave and give up? Fear has started to set into my heart. We have only been married for about three hours now. Saying to myself, "I hope we both heard from God." Tony looked at me and asked, "Are you ok." "Yes, I could not be better," I said. "Why do you look like that?" he asked. I am just a little worried about how things will go from here," I replied. "Let's just enjoy right now and Thank God that we have finally got back on track, "Tony said. "You are right", I said back to him.

Now that we have visited this church with his uncle, the Pastor and his wife seemed very nice. They where rooted deeply in the word of God. We loved the teaching that came from the Man of God. After that one Sunday, we left and went home.

"Tony, did you feel like home at church today?" I asked. "Yes, it felt like a right now word for us," he responded back. "I believe it was, because we needed to hear how to follow through on the vision.", I said. "Let us pray and seek God on, is that the church were He want us to be at? I really don't want us to be out of His will anymore," Tony said. "Yes, I agree with you on that. I do not want to take eight steps backwards when He just took us ten steps forward," I said. Therefore, for a month or so we went to different churches because we both had a Baptist background and we wanted to expand our minds. Unbelievably, every church we went to had some kind of negativity for us to pick out. So we followed God and went back to the church we loved so much. Now we joined and started being activity within the ministry. When you become a couple or even married, you both must seek God and see where you need to be within ministry. The both of you will need to be on a good spiritual level of understanding. As a young married couple fresh back into Christ, we were excited. Also as a young couple that is married, you should sit down and talk about your spiritual needs even before marriage. That way you will know what you are getting into. You both should want just about the same things in life. With Tony and me, we always talked about what we wanted and what we're striving for. Some people do not have a plan laid out, so they start to clash. Not saying that is not your mate from God, but you will have to work a little harder to get things set into place. So please take time out of your busy schedules and talk about these subject matters at hand. So now, I have to learn how to be a great wife. My mother was a single mother and all of my aunts are single as well. I really did not see a married couple much after my grandparents passed away. A wonderful role model that I could remember was my grandparents, but I did not have their advice any more to follow. It was amazing how my husband and I both came from a single parent home. We both had some type of male role model to speak into our lives about skills and knowledge. So now, I have to step into something that I have never seen before or knew how to do. What do I do now? Please don't panic because I did that already! I just had to learn to wait on God and learn from the Bible and go from there. Plus at this church, we had a great example to follow. My mother is a solid Christian woman, but she had a bad marriage so I really could not get much advice from her. Still she gave me some good tips such as, you must stay in the battle and duke it out to the end. To me that was not good advice at the time, because nothing was happening. Nevertheless, little did I know, Tony and I were doing just fine and things seemed well so far. But did the waters rise quickly! Things came so fast and things were happening so fast. The enemy came from all sides seem like. But we stood firm. While I was gone to school Tony would have his own prayer time. We also anointed the house. Once he started that things seemed to get a little smoother. I was going to school full time and going to work full time. I had a lot on my plate. Often Tony and I would sit down and lay things out on the direction God wanted us to go. We wanted a lot but the money was not there. A few months had pasted and I started having some women problems with my body. I had a lot of pain that I have never had before. Prior to this, I went to the doctor and he told me that I was unable to have children. If so, it was going to cost a lot of money to do the different test and treatment even to get pregnant. All of this was told to me before Tony and I got married. Going through that as a woman is very hard. That is all a woman dream of, giving birth to their child or children. Now the enemy had come into my life and took that away from me. So for a little over a year we dealt with that and over came it. We planned when the time is right we would adopt a child. John 10:9-10 states "Yes, I am the gate. Those who come in through me will be saved. Where they go, they will find green pastures. The thief's purpose is to steal kill and destroy. My purpose is to give life in all of its fullness." So for us it was a very hard thing to deal with. Now back to that day of me being in so much pain. It was a Sunday morning and I had a special doctor appointment. He went ahead and ran a pregnancy test on me. Turns out that I am pregnant and the zygote or small baby is not were it should be. This OBGYN tells me that I need to go the hospital and have it removed. I'm in tears, because number one, I am afraid and don't know what is about to happen. Also what do I tell everyone at this time? All these thoughts started racing through my head. I get back to the house so that we can go to church. I told Tony, "lets go and I will tell you what happened on the way." So we get in the car and I start to explain. "Are you in pain right now Nay?" Tony asked, in a sad voice. "Yes I am, but let's just make it to church. I really don't know what to think right now Tony. What are we going to do if I am pregnant? I am not saying lets not have the baby, but money wise," I asked in a concern voice. "Baby, lets just make it to church first and then pray and go from there," Tony said. Well, by the time we got there church was over. Everyone was leaving and we were just trying to get inside the door. Finally, we see the Pastors. I sit down and began to speak with his wife. I really don't know what to say at this point. How do I began, I am thinking to myself? What will she say to me? Fear is all over me. Well, let me calm down first and then I can get my words together. Then Pastor Kim asked me with a soft voice," Are you okay?" "Uhmmm, well, no.", I said quietly. Then I started to explain to her what was going on. Then she said, "so now we need to get you to the hospital." I said softly, "yes." Pastor Daniels was talking to my husband and asking if we wanted to get something to eat. Pastor Kim speaks up and said, "No, Rena needs to go the hospital right now." Pastor Daniels and his wife Pastor Kim went with us and we prayed before we enter into the hospital doors. Let me share right now about these two anointed people from God. They are both very powerful speakers. Pastor Daniels has an anointing to share how to receive from God: faith, favor, and finances unto you in all areas of your life. Pastor Kim is much anointed in prayer, teaching women, healing, and so much more. They had five boys at the time we met them and now they are blessed to have six boys. Better none as "The Legacy". No girls at all! Beautiful children and very well rounded. Now back to the hospital. At this point, the pain was very bad for me. I know that some of it was nerves, because I did not know what to expect. They started the process of calling me in the back and getting a room set up for me. My heart is racing. My hands are sweating very badly. Tony smiled at me and I smiled back. That calmed me down just a little. Then Pastor Kim asked if I was fine? I smiled and said, "Yes for now. The pain has eased a little." Now the nurse calls my name,

"Desiree' Churchman," I raised my hand and I tugged Tony to go with me. He came on and soon as they put me in the room, I asked him to go and get Pastor Kim. I needed a woman by me that was a mother and can pray the devil himself under the bridge. So as the night progressed along, and the tests started, and the results started to come in. "The baby is not were it should be," the doctor said. He started the words surgery to come out of his mouth. I do not want to loose this baby! I thought to myself, my first child and the enemy cannot have it. Pastor Kim prayed and I prayed. As the night went along more test and more results that the doctors had to do. By the end of the night, God had step in right on time. He moved my baby were it needed to be and the doctors were confused. I say we (the praying children of God) were not confused. We all knew that it was God and God alone. This was our, my husband and I first miracle. I cried with joy. I was glad God stepped in on time. Sometimes as a young adult that are saved we forget that we have God on our side. We give up to soon and back out to quick. Sometimes, we forget to call on Jesus. We try to do it ourselves. On that day, we stepped back and let God do the work. I know that it was a blessing that we may share with others, that God is still doing miracles in this day and time. We rejoiced with excitement! The Daniels Family celebrated the news with us as well. I was relieved, but was not at ease at the same time. My mind was saying so much at one time. I had to block that out and move on with my blessing. Through those long nine months, my husband and I grew a lot in all areas of our lives. We were both back active within the church and doing whatever God would have us to do. We loved it. I still went to work and went to school as well. At this point, I changed my major from pharmacy to biology and picked up a minor in chemistry. I pray that I made the right decisions at the time. I will have to stay two - three extra years to do this degree plain, but I will do what I have to do.

    August 19, 2003 at 7:03pm our little miracle daughter was born. Dantionette Tiana Churchman is her name. I was so glad that I had a healthy baby girl. This was a surprise to us, because we did not know what we were having. Two years later another gift from God came. I found out I was pregnant again. I was still in school, working hard with the ministry. We was enjoying every minute of the ministry work. On May 16, 2005, a baby boy arrived healthy as ever. I look at this as God showed man that all things are possible through Him. If you just believe and receive it, God will make it happen for you.

"How do you get things done?" someone asked. Well, get a schedule for yourself. You pray that, certain times should not over flow other important times. As a young woman, I had to learn how to balance things in my life. That is something you will have to learn, it is not given all to you right away. I had to learn that family time is not the same as husband and wife time. Young wives, you cannot use I am tired, headache, don't feel like it 365 days a year! Please ladies, do not act like that is not you, because we all have done it once or twice in our lifetime. Oh, this is the big one! Stop punishing your husband from bedroom time because he has made you mad three days ago. Give your husband a break and have that sweet love time. Learning this you will have to take the time to get to know everything in your schedule. Yes, you may need to know how long you can spend on that one thing at a time. As far as myself, I learned that I could cook and make note cards at the same time. Meaning I was able to put all the food on and while it was cooking I would study. With ministry, you must do the same and balance. Don't give all your time to one thing and forget about the other. The best thing I did was ask God how I should flow with everything. You can never go wrong with asking Him. Look at it as if you are a child and you need some directions on what is needed to be done. It took me a while as a young wife and student at first to get it together. Then I had two small children. "What now!!!," you think. You make it work. We as young women doubt the strength and energy God has given us. We do not put it all to use. With that said, I am still learning how to make the balance work for us as a family. As the years pass on, I know it will only get better as what I am trying to accomplish in life. Things are going okay for our household for the time. Now here comes the enemy. I am thinking to myself this cannot be happening. The trouble seem as though we have no way out. Every bill is past due, our car is messing up, and we have little food in the house. Now what we are going to do? I called Tony at work when things were pressing. "Honey I think they are going to turn the lights off in a couple of days", I said. "How much do we need?" he asked. "To keep them on we need to pay about $100.00," I replied. "I don't know if we have that, let me call you back," he said. Then I blew up! "What do you mean, you have to check about the money?!," I stated. Now ladies I know it sounds like I have lost my mind. Then at the time, I really was stressed and I did not know how to handle my anger. So I had him, my husband to take it out on. THAT IS SO WRONG! Ladies, don't do that at all. That only pushes your husband away from you. But I blew up anyway. Now this is me going smooth off on my husband. "Every time I ask you something, you tell me you don't know, or I will have to check and see." I said with anger in my voice. "Why are you mad or why did your voice changed life that?" he replied in an unease voice. "I don't know, because I am very irritated by how everything is going right now." I said harshly. "Well, Nay I am doing all that I can, and that is it," he said getting upset. I said, "Whatever and I will talk to you later when you get back to me with the needed information." I did not want to pray, I did not want to call on God at this time. Fear is all over me; I am looking at two children and not knowing which way to turn. In the back of my mind, I knew I was wrong, but I was not trying to bring God into it at the moment. Finally my husband called back and said, "Go ahead we have it." I said, "Alright", in a nonchalant tone of voice. "What's wrong baby?" Tony asked. "Nothing," I said. "It's something, because you have been just snapping at me lately," he said. "Nothing is wrong, I'm just tired of not having right now," I said back. "Can we talk about it when I get home from work," he asked. Again, I said to him, "Yeah if you want." At this point, we both should have gone to the Lord. Really, I should have gone to the Lord. That same evening when he arrived home I was asleep. He kissed my forehead and I opened my eyes and spoke very gently to him. "I am sorry that I snapped," I replied. "I really don't know what is going on with me. I just don't like the way things are right now", I stated. "Well I don't either, but things will get better. We have sown seed and we have been tithing to have Gods protection. So things will get better," he replied softly. "I know, it's just getting to that point", I said. Then I asked my husband to forgive me. As young women, we believe that we should have all the answers, and we are never wrong. Well this is a wake up call for you! You will be WRONG, AND YOU DON'T HAVE ALL THE ANSWERS! Let the man be the man of the house. We as young women should follow the Proverbs 31:10-31 woman, a wife of Noble character. I received a great teaching on this same subject at a women's meeting I attend and it was right on time for me.

    Months down the line, we finally broke a cycle that we were in. Every time something came up, we would call on people. This last time we called on God and He brought us out of it. We rejoiced, and identified the cycle that we were in. Thank you Jesus for the learning experience we had. A cycle is, just a learning experience. Some people come out faster than others because they are able to see the cycle and understand the lesson that they need to learn. Some of us stay in the cycle for long periods, because we did not learn everything that was needed to be learned the first time around. Can we still be in the will of

God? Yes, but in order for you to get closer to Him and get the blessing He is trying to give to you, you must learn and come out of the cycle that you are in. Pray and ask God what you need to look for and learn. He will tell you or even show you what the lesson is for you to learn. So I had to do a lot of growing up in the spirit and mentally with some things. I just could not do everything that God has laid out for me. I had that in my mind to do some things and then do the rest on my own. You must follow the plan God has laid out for you so things will go better for you. Please remove the time line of how you want things to go. Don't hinder God from doing His work in your life. He may need you to get married at 21 or 22 years of age. He may have some work for you and your spouse to do. As young adults, we feel this is the time of fun, freedom, and fantasy. The three (F's) can also be done with in God's perfect will for you. Don't think by coming to Christ things are not fun anymore. They just get Better!!!!! So I had to learn all of that and learn it very fast for the sack I wanted this marriage to work. I wanted to show my husband that I was the strong woman God had made me to be. Only he will have to be a little patience with me. Please young people you must have that patience's, because your spouse may not have been in a two parent home. They might not know how a husband should act or treat a wife; he did not see that at home at all. This goes the same with the wife as well. Please don't beat each other up if one came from a single parent home and don't know how a father should treat his kids, or a mother should treat her child, because they have not seen that before in their life. So now, this cycle is being broken with them and they have to learn right along with you. So stand by them and be there for them every step of the way. God will help them in the areas that are needed to be improved on. Again, I say give them the time and let God work, as well as you both must stand by each other firmly.

Our blessing from God was coming soon we both knew it. We just loved the new townhome we were in. Then only a few months there we got a word from God through our pastor, Pastor Daniels that we should look for a house. At the time, we were looking at each other like, we cannot move, but we received the word with an open heart. We really didn't start to look right away.

We did not even know where to start looking. Then after a couple of Sundays went by, we got a word invitation to come look at a house. This amazing couple in the church said to us, "We are selling our house, but come by and take a look at the house." I asked Tony, "Do you want to go and take a look at the house. He said, "Yeah why not." I really don't want to get my hopes all up a then everything falls through again. Here is a side bar, "My husband and I have been praying and searching for a house that will be large enough so that we will be comfortable, and be able to meet the need of someone that needed somewhere to stay. We would be able to open our doors and welcome them in. So now, a lot has happened and we have been turned away, so many times I really did not know what to do at this point. Now this family was saying come in and see our home and let's talk. We said okay and went over the same day. In my mind, I did not want to put all my heart into this. We as young women need to know for sure about things. If we do not have the, who, what, when and where, even who will it affect, then we shy away from it. Young women do not like giving their hearts if they are afraid or do not know the out come up front. As saved young women we must step out on faith. In Matt. 21:21-22 said; Then Jesus told them, " I assure you, if you have faith and don't doubt, you can do things like this and much more. You can even say to this mountain, "May God lift you up and throw you into the sea, "and it will happen. If you believe, you will receive, what ever you ask for in prayer." Young women as you read this remember this in your hearts. I know it will be some hard moments that arise but go back to this scripture and it will help you every time. Plus trust your husband and pray that he hears from God with the directions he is moving the family in. Well, with me I just set back and listen to everything that the couple had to say. I did not respond to much. I did say I love the house. My husband and I got back to our house with the normal routine. The kids eating dinner, taking their baths, then pray, and going to bed, then off to sleep they will go. Alright, we have a two year old and the baby boy that was about six months old. So you know it was a lot more than just off to sleep at that time for them two. But it sounded good to imagine. Anyway, we sat down and Tony asked me what I thought. I said, "Well I don't want to get all excited and then my heart get broken." "Don't think like that Nay, just trust me on this, and we will get through. Baby, this might be our season to get a home. The children will need space and the yard.", Tony shared. "I know but, I don't think I can go through this. What if?," I started to say. "Don't say it," Tony said with a little aggression. "Say what?!" I replied quickly. "Don't say anything negative right now. Do not even say that you don't think you can go through this right now. All I want you to say is, I trust you and that's all." Tony said. Ladies at this point, I wanted to say some unsaved words to him. My flesh was fighting to come unglued. All kinds of thoughts were flying in my mind. "Are you mad now?", Tony asked. I said, "Calmly, NO, I am not." Now ladies we know that we are mad. Ladies we're looking crazy with our eyebrows dented in, sharp answers, or the famous quiet treatment. Plus the number one killer is, No more love making for two days, or whatever time line we are on. Some set the time on how mad we are. Ladies we must stop the Drama! We as women must first stop lying to ourselves, and to our husbands. I know I was mad, but I did not want the argument to get worse. So I said no. Ladies even though we are mad don't take that special moment away from each other. I know you are thinking what I am talking about. I am saying that when you take something away you take it from the both of you. You are thinking that you are hurting him, but you are hurting yourself as well. Now he is upset with you, and trying to get back at you. Don't put your relationship with your spouse in that kind of drama. Just tell them to let you calm down first. Never go to sleep upset or angry with your spouse. The enemy will come in and now your guard is down. So, I just got really quiet. After some hours pasted, and God convicted me about not trusting my husband, I did not want to hear that at this time. God showed me, a clip of what could happen in my life if I kept bringing non-trust spirits into our relationship. He, (God) showed me the spirit kept growing until it was fully-grown. It over took my relationship and destroyed it. I could not breathe after the vision; I could not even move a muscle. Tony walked in the room and sat on the bed. He looked very frustrated and hurt. Then he spoke to me very softly. "Are you ready to speak to me now?" I said, "Yes with a half smile on my face." He told me to come close to him and I did very, very slow. I sat by him and before he could say a word, I said, "I am very sorry for not putting my all into your decision. I know that I need to trust you on this. You may be right. I put doubt and untrust in my heart. My flesh was jumping around and I did not know what to do. I am very sorry and will you forgive Me.," I asked. "Yes, I will, but do you understand what I was saying or not," he asked. Let me tell you a little about Tony. After he has said something and he knows in his heart that it is right, he wants to make sure that you understand everything that he was trying to say. That's the kind of heart God gave him. So my answer to him was, "yes, I do understand. I love you so much, and I don't want you to forget that," I said to him. He said, "I love you too." "May I have a hug from you?" I asked. "Yes you may," he responded with a smile. After we have a disagreement, we always hug to seal the deal or everything is back and better than before. If you disagree with your spouse and once you both get back on the same page, you both should be different for the better. That is one more thing you have over come together. I was once taught to fight with the heart, not the body. Once I put that into play, some arguments would not blow up to the full bomb. They stay in or under management. By reading this, I pray that you will take note of that and watch how much easer to resolve the problem at hand.

From that day on my personal prayer was let the seeds we have sown come forth in a great harvest. By October 2005, the blessing came forth. The Gaskin Family blessed us. We were able to move into the house. We were able to set a payment amount and some more important things. We knew it was God, because who else could have made it possible. All the bills started to line up for us. All we could say was, Thank You God. This Family could not have come into our lives at a better time. Not for the house, but because we all needed to have some type of impact on each other lives. You think to yourself what can a young couple with two small children impact a couple that has been together for more than 24 years. I don't know, but God is making it possible. Some times people just need to see how God can work in your life no matter how old you are. Praise the Lord in all you do and He will continue to bless you for all the days to come. Our Family is a living witness to that.

My Scripture and Prayer

Isaiah 26:1-4 (The New Living Translation)

In that day, everyone in the land of Judah will sing this song:

Our city is now strong!

We are surrounded by the walls of God's Salvation.

Open the gates to all who are righteous; allow the faithful to enter. You will keep in perfect place all who trust in you, whose thoughts are fixed on you! Trust in the Lord always, for the Lord God is the eternal Rock.

My Prayer: (Pray this Prayer)

Father God, I thank you for all the harvest that has came forth. Thank you for allowing certain, and the right people to be in contact with my family and I . Let my flesh continue to die unto the spirit man. Let me continue to fight with the heart and not with the flesh, Lord God. Let my husband and I get to the root of the problem instead of letting the enemy run a ring around us. Let my husband hear closely to you Father God, let all the negativity be stopped before entering into his ears and eyes Father. Let our marriage grow stronger and closer not only together but more so unto you Father. I thank you for favor and allowing Blessing to come unto us. Let the blessing flow above and beyond so that we may be able to bless those that have a need. Restore unto those that have given unto us Father, bless their household and let their harvest come forth. I thank you and I give you all the praise and all the glory. In the name of Jesus, I pray:

Amen

Comments/Notes:

_____

_____

_____

_____

~The Vision God Gave Me ~

~The Vision God Gave Me ~

Since my husband and I have been together I always would fix some type of dessert, and I loved it to no end. I enjoyed watching others indulged themselves in the desserts. It was my joy. I felt like I had blessed someone with something that they did not like fixing themselves, but enjoyed eating. So I prayed to God. Then within a few weeks later I just sat down and started writing. God put in my heart what I needed to do. The word of God said, write the vision and make it plain. So I did just that. My biggest thing was who will buy these items from me? Everybody is telling me to make the price at this rate then the next person will say this rate. Some said make them very expensive, and some real cheap. I had so much advice on what to do and the direction I should take. So I started to make a small or should I say a growing menu. Then before long, I had a company name. "_**Sweet Dreams TX Style**_" (elegant southern pastries and so more.) Now my company name was set in place. Then before long, a price list and creative ideas started to roll for me. Now over the past few years, I have also had some ups and downs. I have also learned that I must follow the first vision God gave me. Every time I step in and try something new without God telling me first, it failed big time. Not that it was not a good idea but not the right time for it. When God gives you something, first take it like you are pregnant. First, start with all light and healthy things to feed your vision. For example, pray over the vision, read the word of God, and start giving God the praise for it. Now take note of this before I move on; if you don't get up to do it, the vision will not be held up. God will move to someone else and the work will get done. Please be the willing vessel that God needs. Now back to the growing vision. Be very careful to whom you share your vision with. This can be very harmful if they bring a lot of doubt, and negativity unto your vision. This may cause your vision to die or be killed. So you must protect your vision as if it was your first trimester of your pregnancy. Then keep feeding it as it shall grow. Wait until God assures you before the vision is birth out unto the world. Sow seed for your vision as well. I did all these things for my vision. I listened to

God and took other opinions into consideration. Every ne that I came in contact with, wanted to be apart of this company some kind of way. I had so many helping hands that wanted to help, but some did not want their hands to get dirty.

Now I can really say since my company has taken off in this past year of 2006, God has placed an awesome woman of God right by my side. She always says it is your idea, I just help. Sometimes God will place a vessel that sees your vision and will help you put it out to the world. I love you Gwen Gaskin for all you have done! I thank God for you. Now back to the vision. You must let the person God has sent to you do his or her role. If not some things will be put to a stop. Remember you cannot handle everything on your own, so just relax and let them do their part. As for me, I was happy because I did not know how to put some things into play. My helping hands, this is a partner more than just helping hands to me. Gwen helps keep me on the right path, very honest with me and do not let me jump into the deep end. Thank you Jesus, because I know that I will. I still have some of the vision that has not come to past, but I know that it is coming soon. With all that said, just hang in there, and don't give up! Let God guide you and lead you with the vision He gave you. Will you be a millionaire? Not that instance, but who is to say you will not be. But keep believing in God on the level you want your vision on. In the book of Proverbs, it said to frame your world with the words of your mouth. So say and confess the kingdom of God. When you put the kingdom of God first in building your business or whatever your vision God has given you, it will go above and beyond what you have ever imagined. Even with the vision of my book, I had to follow the same steps, but a little closer for it to come to pass. A wise man once told me that, "If you believe in God and within your heart anything is possible for you to tackle and handle." I took that and put that effort of applying my all unto God, and He made all the rest happen for me. So to see the things and skills God has blessed my hands and the anointing He has on me, take a look at my website: www.sweetdreamstxstye.com! Place an order or even just contact me for yourself.

So now, get up off of your blessed assurance and write

down the vision, and seek the wisdom of God, and go for it. I'm not a multimillionaire just yet, but I know it is coming unto me! So if I can do it, I know anyone in the world can do it as well. You don't have to have a lot of money, but you need a lot of Jesus Christ, faith, and patience. So go now in the name of Jesus and do what God has placed on your heart.

My Scripture and Prayer:

Proverbs 3:1-6 (The New Living Translation)

My child, never forget the things I have taught you. Store my commands in your heart, for they will give you a long and satisfying life. Never let loyalty and kindness get away from you! Wear them like a necklace; write them deep within your heart. Then you will find favor with both God and people, and you will gain a good reputation. Trust in the Lord with all your heart do not depend on your own understanding. Seek his will in all you do, and he will direct your path.

Pray this Prayer:

Father God I want to thank you for all you have giving me with this vision. Please help me understand each and every detail that you have given me. Let me hear clearly from you for when the time is right for it to be birth. Let my spiritual ears be blocked from all negative and ungodly advice. Let all my finances line up according to your will Father God. Let my church, business, and schooling be what you will have it to be. By me having this vision Father God is first to build up your kingdom. Let favor and all things that is needed to be with in my pathway. Let me stay focus and not stray off the vision pathway or even your path Father God. Please guide me back on track if I do get off track. Let me have an open and willing heart when you send me people or persons to help me fulfill the vision. Let this vision be guidance to you Father God. Let it become a full-blown ministry for me to witness to people and lead them to you. I thank you in all I do and I magnify your name Father God. In the name of Jesus, I pray: Amen

Comments/Notes

_____

_____

_____

_____

_____

~ *My Thoughts, Comments, and Encouragements*~

~ My Thoughts, Comments, and Encouragements~

Encouragements:

I would first like to say: I hoped you have enjoyed what you have just read. I pray this book has made a difference to occur in your life, and only for the better. I hope that if you were not saved you got saved through this book. I pray that you find a great bible teaching church, and you fulfill your ministry and the work God has for you. If you were saved reading this book: I pray it has taken you to another level spiritually, and mentally, and stirred up your gifts within. Stay focus and keep your mind on God. Don't let the enemy come in and overtake you. Please don't rely upon your people to pull you through all the storms. Count on God and He will bring you through them all. Keep praying and studying the word of God, and give Him all the praise. Be wise in all the people that you let surround you. Remember this will not be an easy walk, but you still may have lots of fun within this walk. Don't let others tell you that you cannot laugh and enjoy yourself in Christ, because you can. Wait on God before you make a move in any direction of your life. Parents keep your child or children in the word. Hear them out on whatever it is they have to say. Don't over react to some things that they tell you, but handle it with the right punishment if needed, or embrace them.

If you are married, keep your house in order. Ladies anoint the house and set the mood, also remember that your husband is the head of the household. Learn to fight with the heart and get to the bottom of the problem instead of the flesh. Don't let the enemy come in and break up something God has put together. Expect a blessing daily to come in your household. Also, ladies stay honest with yourselves and even with your husbands. I encourage you to follow your heart and most of all follow God. Proverbs 16:3; Commit to the Lord whatever you do, and your plans will succeed.

Thoughts:

I believe by writing and obeying God that my life as been

elevated. Spiritually my mind has gone to a higher dimension. In writing this book, it has pulled a lot of things out of me. Some of the abilities I did not know I ever had. I did not believe that I would ever have time to do this book, but God had plans and made the time happen for me. I just wonder what else God has for me? What else could be unlocked to come out? This book has made me see some things that I did pay a lot of attention to. Meaning, some of my characters about myself that I needed too still work on, God smooth them out during the process of this book. Therefore, that will let you know that no one is perfect, but God is perfecting us all.

      Thank you Jesus!

Comments:

      The comments that I have is, get ready for whatever God is about to do in your life. No matter what age range or group you are in, just get ready. Let the gift flow out of you like never before. He will only do what your heart is open and willing for

Him to use. So just, open your heart and step out on faith and GET BLESSED!

May God bless you and go forth with your vision. Remember God is with you all the way. Just remember to tackle yourself first and let Him work inside out!

My Personal Scripture:

My heart took delight in all my work, and this was the reward for all my labor...

Ecclesiastic 2:10

My Personal Prayer:

Father God, thank you for opening my heart and eyes to hear and see the vision that you laid out for me. I thank you for blessing my hands to write this book. I pray that everyone reading this book will see what you have for them and run with the vision Father God. I pray this book will be a blessing to each and every one that reads this book and have a life changing experience! In the name of Jesus I pray

Amen

Now say a prayer for yourself and the level you want to go to! With this prayer, it will end the book, but open a new beginning chapter for what God has for you.

BE BLESSED!

THE BEGINNING

~ NOT ~

THE END

~The Author~

Desiree' Churchman was born in Tyler, Texas and now a resident of Houston, Texas. A Reverends wife and a mother of three wonderful children, Dantoinette, Dantione II, and Dristen. She is also a growing business owner and graduate of Texas Southern University. Desiree' received a B.S. in Biology and a minor in chemistry. Striving for what God has for her, and sharing the knowledge, that He has placed in her heart. All of that said, to say an awesome Woman of God!

~Upcoming Titles~

"Where is Jesus? The Adventures of D.J."

Written by: Desiree' Churchman

Illustrations by: Ricky Gaskin

This book is about a little boy trying to find the best gift to give to his uncle, which is Jesus.

A great children's book to read to your child or children.

"Our Relationship"

Compiled by: Desiree' Churchman

This book is about different types of relationships, and how it affected your relationship with God.

Look for the release dates or when our release dates was on www.ladiesofpower.weebly.com under the Product Tab.

~Notes~

www.ingramcontent.com/pod-product-compliance
Lightning Source LLC
Chambersburg PA
CBHW020917090426
42736CB00008B/680